Microcosm Publishing is Portland's most diversified publishing house and distributor with a focus on the colorful, authentic, and empowering. Our books and zines have put your power in your hands since 1996, equipping readers to make positive changes in their lives and in the world around them. Microcosm emphasizes skill-building, showing hidden histories, and fostering creativity through challenging conventional publishing wisdom with books and bookettes about DIY skills, food, bicycling, gender, self-care, and social justice. What was once a distro and record label was started by Joe Biel in his bedroom and has become among the oldest independent publishing houses in Portland, OR. We are a politically moderate, centrist publisher in a world that has inched to the right for the past 80 years.

CONTENTS

CREDITS

As always, in the final moments of wrapping up yet another zine I'm thinking of my friends who make my life rich and full and whom I could never thank enough for all their love and support. It would take pages to acknowledge them all and a "credits" section needs and wants to be specific. First of all: much on-going appreciation to the Big Yella House collective for their gift of the Hobos from Hell office, without which, this zine would not exsist. Also, without the massive generosity of my european friends and relatives the subject matter of "Eurohobo...." would only be a fantasy. Big appreciation to Aunt Rosemary, cuzins Carol and Georges. And Raymonde and Alex. And the rest of the "Lutry gang". Big thanx to Kathy and Sam, squatter friends in London. Gilad and Neus in Barcelona. Heather number one in Athens. Martin and Veann in Muhldorf. Thanx, Shreya, who travelled with me for a month in Spain. Fellow traveller, Janni, in germany... and others.

Most of the photos in here are mine, borrowed a few from varios sources, but I wanted to thank so much Steffan for both his inspiration and his two shots in here. Also, big thanx for the pix in here taken by fellow eurohobos, Gilad and Heather Adams/Agular. I borrowed the funny phrase "How do you say 'hump yard' in german?" from my friend, Brakeshoe. Micheal of G.I.O. and Grundig fame gave editing and proof reading advice for which I'm much indebted and because of whom I have a slightly better grasp of comma usage. Thanx, Shreya for the beautiful hoboerotica. Mucho thanx to Jason for tech printing support.

Welcome to "Eurohobo"– a zine about travelling the motherlands "on pennies a day" as old travel guidebooks from the 60s and 70s would've put it. The world has become a more expensive place since then. Three dollar hotel rooms in mexico twenty years ago, go for twenty now. A cup of coffee in paris will put you out 3 bucks. What if, by being thrifty, "scam wise", and "hobocore", one could travel in europe as cheaply as in asia, africa, or south america?

Prior to Heather number two and mine journey in '98, I'd only known one hobo friend to successfully hop freights in europe and his story inspired us to try. We flew across the big water for under 500 bucks, slept on the streets of paris, hitchhiked around, visited friends and relatives, and whetted our appetites for train hopping there, all on a low budget. For the big trip of '05, four hundred and sixty seven dollars got me there and back thanx to a patient computer friend and an internet "off season" flight. A thousand dollars earned on a month long carpentry job was my spending money stashed in my boots (hobo style). Six months later, a lonely twenty spot got me from airport to home and a burrito into the belly.- I'd managed to average around two hundred a month. Staying in squats in london, camping in caves and orchards in spain, sleeping in factories, freight yards and ditches all over. Dumbsters, both lavish and meager. The kindness of friends with guest beds and hot meals and a bike to borrow in barcelona and athens and canton bern. The overwhelming and sweet kindness of my swiss family, a lovers dorm room in england. These all helped stretch the budget and more precious; emotionally balanced out the lean (and occasionally, lonely) nights and days on the road. I tried to give back dumbstered wealth, scam and hobo knowledge, my carpentry skills and friendship. Besides dumbsters (plentiful and overflowing in some countries) and camping out, train scams and freight train riding were the preferred low-bag mainstays.

Combined, the two euro tours added up to 23 freight trains in six countries and five times that many passenger trains in nine countries (only a few of which were paid for). Hopping freights thru "the chunnel"(under the english channel) and tramping eastern europe/russia remain unfulfilled dreams (next time?) but were sweetly compensated by crossing the alps three times by freight, and three other mountain ranges (the jura, pyrenees, and the appenino), as well the coasts of spain, france, and italy. Regardless of the sheer hard work of train hopping there and occasional crappy luck, not a day went by without some moment of self reflection, agrin would break out: "Wow, I'm a hobo in europe...I'll be remembering this!" This zine is an attempt to pass on both the inspiration (or is it foolishness?) as well as the practical "how-to" stuff. How-to info gets boring, so hopefully some of the stories will add some spice. Enjoy!

JURA MOUNTAIN HOP

Would we be seen yet again? Heather number two and mine luck, so far, had sucked! A half dozen nights of getting on the inside, slinking and sneaking, sleeping and waiting in as many freight yards had all been in vain. A perplexed and mildly amused pair or french yard workers, one of whom we figured to be a supervisor type, had kicked our stowaway asses off an auto rack train. Cold feet and last minute indecision lost us another train out of Paris....was it the armed, roaming train station guards who looked ready to maybe shoot anything out of the ordinary (train station bombings have been reality in europe, decades before americans ever had a serios thot about terrorism). The dijon freight yards hadn't worked out for us either. While scouting and checking out freight car destination placards in a busy, well lit yard in southern switzerland I'd gotten seen and confronted by five or six mystified workers. Sans french, my pantomime of what I was doing there and what we wanted (a westbound train) quickly devolved into a joke. Heather and I were still new to the concept (but catching on) of hobos not being a concept, as exemplified by these workers scratching their heads. Plus the

language thing. Toward the end, in desperation, I turned around in mid-sentence, trying to show off the faded punk patch on my hoodie, a graphic of some kids on an american boxcar. "See, see! Train du merchandise, westbound!" It didn't work. I guess I'd become the wingnut of the week, an american one, no less, in that freight yard. Absurd and frustrating. I bid a quick au revoir and scurried off to Heather hiding with the packs in the trackside bushes, "Shit, we gotta get outta here, I think they're gonna call security." We hadn't moved an inch, much less, a kilometer on a freight train yet.

Now, a hitchhiking day later, up in the mountains, a charming swiss train station, crossing our fingers on a grainer porch, crouching shadows, ready to depart westbound. We're sandwiched between an active passenger train that has just pulled in and a station platform. A worker walks by tapping each car with a hammer, he's singing "I Walk The Line" in french, blind to us. We're paranoid, a familiar feeling, how is it that the station passengers don't see us? Moments of nervous invisibility, but determined...we've paid our dues and nothing to loose! Then, just like that, we're off, quickly leaving the station

behind. Within a moment our speed is crazy fast, the roar is deafening! Laughing, gesturing, talking is out of the question. Finally-- our first freight train in europe! Instantly, everything goes dark, for long moments we dare not move for fear of tumbling off the porch. Somewhere in here, in what we estimate must be a ten mile long tunnel, we cross (illegally) into france. Out the other end, we ride thru the Jura mountains, in glorious bloom, it's May. It just became all well worth it! We grin at each other. ###

EUROHOBO: (HANDY STUFF TO KNOW)

Freight hopping in western europe is hard work! By that, I mean, by comparison to hoboing in northamerica-likely its the trickiest and toughest way to travel europe with the possible exceptions being boat and ship hopping/ferry ride scams(if such things exist?)Is it worth the time and trouble and energy? Depends on who you are and what you wanna see and experience? If you are enamoured with freight trains and like to ride them,and can sustain stubborn(bordering on obsessive) qualities ,you'll go far and see much.Often.especially when the luck was running thin,a certain stubborn "hang-in-thereness" went a long ways for me. Why ride freights when you can fly for cheap,bike tour,hitch hike("auto stop" as its universally known by here),ride the ferries, rent a car,or ride "the plush"-those plentiful passenger trains? Depending on the time you have,yur itenerary and goals, you'll do a fair bit of some or even all of those other modes of travel. As it is anywhere in the world that freight trains exsist,tramping europe has it's own unique flavors and to become a hobo here,is in many ways, to play a differnt game.I'll leave it to others,more articulate and poetic than I,to describe the joys and beauty of euro train hopping: there's plenty of both! Some of the fun (and work) of doing the steel-on-steel thing here are the many notable and important differences and challenges.

As follows,in no particular order(except as it made sense to me) are the obvious and sometimes,subtle distinctions of riding the rails "Eurohobo" style.

ELECTRIC

predominates here (the one exception I saw in my travels was Greece, where trains are diesel and train routes,few). It was amazing, to me, the complexity of the infrastucture- millions of kilometers of over-head wire and their supporting towers,power stations, etc. There was something repeatedly hypnotic in staring up, while riding along at high speeds,at what I can only describe as "the weaving of the lines". Exceptions are some yard dogs(switch engines)which can work the parts of freight yards that dont have the electric lines and the occasional non-electric route(for instance I rode a couple of diesel trains in some desert mountains of Spain). The electric wires provide power to the locomotives and hang only a few feet above the freight cars; common sense and a big warning sign on some freight car ladders will remind you of the danger. The common N.american tactic of climbing up for an overview of the yard,scouting where the head end of the train is at,what's happening 3 tracks over, etc. I treated with extreme caution -never taking my eyes off the overhead wires while climbing ladders and always staying several feet below the wire. With the exception of the top deck of auto racks, riding on top of freight cars should be an obvious no-no! Even on non-electric routes trains can and do merge without warning or stopping onto overhead wired tracks. My guess is a single touch to these wires (30,000 volts?) is tramp barbeque- tramp being the main course. Beware!

TRAIN WORKERS,

as much as I was able to determine, are completely or mostly unfamiliar with rail riders, whom are rare or non-existant (in western europe). This is due to several factors;

a different and older history of migrant labor patterns, poverty, and union organizing and how these don't correspond to train riding subculture as they do in north america, as well as just the ease of riding the ubiquitous and pletiful passenger trains, even without money.

Also, I noticed some somewhat subtle and residual guilt in parts of europe about freight trains and their part in the death camps: boxcars are not for people transport! The upside of all this, when seen by workers and security, is it's easy to pretend(when yur not on a train, of course) that yur

lost from the passenger station,or camping or sightseeing or railfaning(yes,it exists in europe)or just cutting across the yard. The downside is it can be difficult,sometimes impossible,to find accurate or detailed information from yard and train workers. Culture and language barriers can further hinder information gathering.Nonetheless,when seen,don't discount working class solidarity and sympathy which can include friedliness,curiosity, and helpfulness on their part.Respond in kind.As many times as not, when I was seen,workers turned a blind eye to me,or were curios and helpful when they could have just as easily kicked me off or called train security,etc. Train workers in many places wear brightly colored overall type uniforms(blue,orange,etc.it varied from country to country) or at the very least,bright colored safety vests,which makes it harder for the hobo to blend in.Also, euro yards often have a much higher population of workers than their american counterparts.For that reason I tended to prefer smaller,less industrial and less well lit yards. Big or small, I constantly relied on my stealth and hobo_ninja skills here. Of all the factors,the "worker thing" may be the single largest glaring difference you'll encounter in europe.

TUNNELS:

Europeans are crazy about them, many of which are the longest in the world! If there's a hill or a mountain in the way, they most likely have gone right thru it, or with the English channel, right under it; "the chunnel" and yes, it runs freight. With the exception of diesel routes, they are smoke free. Often, well lit and double track. Exhilarating!

entering a tunnel on a piggyback
austria

YARDS:

The configuration of freight yards, signals, switching, yard clearance, towers, switch engines, crew changes, etc. are all more or less similar to the states, canada, & mexico but with notable exceptions, one being more so here; freight yards and passenger stations/passenger train yards are often close together, sometimes even one and the same. Though, some big cities have their big yards out in the boonies and you can waste a lotta time and energy futzing around inner city yards when where you might wanna be is somewhere out in the country at the big yards. Catching out at or near large and small passenger stations can work well for both originating and thru trains. Freight stops at passenger stations can be regular or random and often are brief, sometimes only for a few seconds or minutes at most, sometimes longer. I caught many trains from stations, day and night, needless to say, night time is best for sustainable stealth and waiting.

SECURITY:

is prevalent at train stations and of some concern to the rail rider. Alertness, discretion, timing, hiding, blending in, dark clothes, and night time slinking are all important elements. When those fail or they might arouse unneccesary suspicion and/or sometimes in the daytime I found the blatant "go for it" and the "don't mind me. I belong here" approach to work well... certainly not unfamiliar tactics for north american riders. Sometimes security (as everywhere) is inattentive or even "blind" because, well, train stations are busy places; travellers, punks, and backpacks don't neccesarily stand out and remember, hoboing is virtually unknown here. Security and railroad police are not looking for riders-they are looking for terrorists, theives, trouble makers and probably most commonly, low-lifes hanging out. It's not unusual to see people short cutting across the freight/passenger train yards, walking their dogs, etc. At night if yur scouting and stash yur pack, you can pass as a worker from a distance, less so in the day, since it seems to be universal that all train workers wear bright colored uniforms or safety vests. Don't forget the old "I'm a dumb american, I don't know the language (even if you do)" foreigner priveledge thing that can go a long ways toward light and easy encounters on or off the trains. Myself, being kicked off fright trains 3 or 4 times by workers but never busted by cops, its difficult to say what the worst case scenario might be for freight riding? Possible legal or quasi legal consequences might be infraction tickets? Bribes? Jail time? Court appearences? Deportation? Hanging? (just joking, ha ha). Encounters and consequences probably vary from country to country, situation to situation, eastern versus western europe, private security or city police or railroad cops, etc. The on-going impression for me is that north americanos carry a fair bit of priveledge here and a lecture, a finger wagging ("Verboten!") and possibly an infraction (you'll never pay!) will be the most yur likely to encounter. Do be ready to show yur passport or "papers" as they say in some places. Play it innocent and friendly, play it cool!

DETAILS:

Much of both the larger and finer points that we take for granted are quite different here. Stirrups, steps, ladders, grab irons, catwalks, and handrails all exist but will seem unfamiliar and often poorly positioned and much skimpier than we're used to, sometimes dangerously skimpy, making it harder for on the fly moves, crossing trains in freight yards, etc. Couplings are a very different hook and latch system along with a funny dual bumper design. Slack action is non-existant, and so, with no pinching movement in the couplings, one can, when neccesary and with caution and good handholds, cross strings of cars by stepping on the bumpers and couplings. Freds (flashing rear end devices) come singly or in pairs, depending on the country, sometimes they blink, sometimes not. They are lightweight boxes that tend to be put on and off the tail end quickly and without much ado, and often (not always) at the last moment, making it sometimes harder to "read" the direction of the trains while scoping out big yards. As with everything, there are common exceptions and I did find freds to be of occassional help on figuring out the direction of a train and/or it's readiness to depart.

stirrups and steps can be skimpy

hook and latch coupling

flashing rear end devices, grainer porch, france

a mercedez benz auto rack train, northern italy

SPEED & SIZE:

You can certainly find yurself on a slow freight but that's more the exception. Most, even short distance, trains move at high speeds, scary fast and exhilarating! Start ups, slow downs and stops happen very quickly and quietly due to being electric powered and they carry much lighter loads. Most freight cars are small and carry less weight. Ten to thirty freight cars long is the average and forty is a long train, which makes walking and cutting around strings of cars in yards easier but placement is trickier when yur waiting as trains are very short. Catching on the fly or while stopped is often limited to a time window of seconds, as crew changes, station stops, signal stops, yard clearence, siding meets and even yard switching can happen quickly. Whole yards can empty out in hours, one train after another, minutes apart, if it's a busy yard, intermingled with thru freights and the ever constant passenger trains. The briskness of euro rails make north american freights seem slow, ponderous, and heavy. One american hobo friend described his feelings, after a few rides, as "like riding on toy trains". They are, nonetheless, fast, serious, and just as potentially dangerous, often requiring quick and even, impulsive "go for it" decisions. The relative quietness of the trains, the high speeds, and the frequency of passenger trains make it vital to be attentative when crossing tracks, hanging out, cutting around the ends of trains in yards and sidings, trying to catch on the fly, etc. European passenger trains reach speeds of 200 mph and freights, half that. They are electric, fast, and quiet, beware!

###

EUROPEAN FREIGHT CARS

There's a huge variety of freight car design in europe: in the style, length, and size, much more so than in north america. Many freight cars are quite short and compact and others, as long as we're familiar with. Most only have four wheels but you'll occasionally see cars with 8 wheels. To add complexity to the mix, freight car designs vary from country to country. As follows are the varios types of cars and their qualities and limitations as regards commoness, rideability, hideability, and weather protection, etc.....a general and specific (but not neccesarily comprehensive) guide. If yur serious about euro train hopping, keep yur eyes open for the sweet variety of available rides here, mix and match and be creative.

empty auto rack, swiss alps

inside a mercedez benz, auto rack train, italy

AUTO RACKS
(AUTOMOBILE CARRIERS)

North american riders, you'll think you died and went to hobo heaven. Quite common, a wide variety of auto racks, most commonly two decks but sometimes just one. Either full or empty these are excellent for riding. All are open ended, some are enclosed with wire mesh or opaque plastic, some, wide open. All are inviting. You can be selective on which ones offer the most hiddeness for yur situation. Sometimes the cars inside are unlocked which makes for an even more comfortable and hidden ride. If you do ride inside, try and leave the car as undisturbed as possible for yur own protection (case you get caught later on, on or near the train) and to not set a precedent. Also, be careful to not open a car door that's faced the wrong way- the wind could rip it and damage the door. If the doors are locked or the rack is empty you'll just have to brave it out in the open, either on the top deck or the lower deck. Even loaded with (locked) cars, wind protection is minimal, be prepared.

motion, empty auto rack

BOXCARS:

Again as with other european freight cars, there's a huge variety of types and sizes. Small oldish looking wooden boxcars, canvas and metal "covered wagon" style boxcars, long ones, short ones, even a "telescoping" kind, etc. Unfortunatly, it's rare to see an open boxcar, forget riding inside but there's a few kinds that offer decent rides (though exposed to weather and being seen) on one end - a catwalk with decent handrails. You can occasionally find open abandoned boxcars that offer good camping and waiting spots.

some boxcars have small platforms on one end that are rideble, swiss boxcar

swiss military train

COIL CARS

Easily recognizable, not especially hidden but rideable full or empty.

FLAT CARS

A variety of non container style flat cars exist with the usual exposure to view and weather, more hidden when they're carrying trucks-piggy back style, military vehicles, track machinery, farm tractors, etc.

FLATS WITH CONTAINERS/ BULK TANKERS/ TRUCKS

A lot of euro traffic consists of these. As you might guess, flats are often the high priority cargo along with auto racks and you can trust them to do longer, sometimes, multi-country distance rides. Unfortunatly, "48 well type" cars are uncommon(see "WELL CARS"). If you ride containers, bulk tankers, or trucks(piggy back style), you'll most likely end up on a flat with a wide variety of design and style, and how they configure together. Rideability can be cramped or spacious, usually fairly exposed to view and weather, the most hidden when under a truck on a flat.

container flat, spain

low walled flat with container

In some countries, containers are commonly put onto what I would call "low walled flats"(18 inch high walls) which offer a somewhat more hideable ride. Wasn't common but occasionally you'd see scrap metal or rock being carried on these.

GRAINERS (CLOSED HOPPER CARS)

grainer porch, italy

type of grainer, france

Grainers come in a large variety of design and are, along with container flats, one of the most common rides and one of the best hidden on spacious porches on either end. Generally, they tended to be high priority freight, that is, fast, whether doing long distance or short distance.

GONDOLAS

Similar to north american gondolas they carry metal, scrap, etc. Rideable with the usual precautions-shifting loads, etc.

grainer porch, switzerland

LOCOMOTIVES

four types of locomotives, lausanne train station, switzerland

Mostly electric, occasional diesel. They come in different styles in different countries, old ones,new ones, sometimes interchangeable for pulling freight or passenger. They often have cabs at either end,no external walkways. With the exceptions of especially fast and/or heavy trains or steep mountain grades,there's usually only one unit per train,which makes locomotive rides sketchy and unlikely. I never felt even remotely tempted to ride them in europe.

OPEN TOP HOPPER CARS (COAL CARS,ROCK, DIRT & GRAVEL CARS)

swiss gravel car

There are dozens of types and almost all to varying degrees, offer hideable and spacious porches to ride with some decent protection from weather and being seen. If yur trying to be especially covert, of course there's always riding up in the rock, gravel, or coal(dirty!) They can be damnably slow,low priority trains but I had some fast ones, as well.

PASSENGER TRAIN AUTO RACKS

In some countries,occasional high class,fast passenger trains have auto racks(automobile carriers) attached. You'll surely need that beemer while sunbathing Monaco,eh?! For us lower classes, this can be the fast, multi-country short or long ride we're looking for. These are fast high-priority trains; stealth and hobo ninja skills required! Usually the top deck is the most hidden but has minimal wind protection at high speeds...remember these are passenger trains that can reach speeds in excess of a 100 MPH, or more. Asking at train stations, calling, or finding the right brochure can give you info on where and when passenger trains with rideable auto racks do their thing.

SWITCH ENGINES

They come in a large variety of designs. The same as in the states, "yard dogs" are the work engines of the freight yards, making up and breaking up trains. Some are electric, some are diesel. Also, similar to the states, over-the-road locomotives are sometimes used in the yards to move freight around, as well.

switch engine, spain

empty low walled flat with swiss switch engine in background

TANKER CARS

The highly desperate ride of north america, here are invitingly rideable and relatively hideable on large porches, decks, or at the very least, large end catwalks with handrails. Many designs and styles.

tanker car porch, switzerland

WELL CARS

(TANKS IN A BUCKET, PIGS IN A BUCKET)

Though not particularly common, keep yur eyes open for these- possibly the most hidden and weather proof of euro freight cars: high -priority "well" type

hidden in a well car, france

cars with the wells in the middle and are rideable empty or full. They can carry trucks (a cramped ride) or bulk tankers (a spacious ride). Riding empties, yur still somewhat hidden from view but exposed to weather.

under a bulk tanker on a well car, french nuclear power plant in the background

truck on a flat (piggy back style)

austria

TACTICS, STRATEGIES, AND A FEW HELPFUL TIPS

MAPS:

I've never been so immersed into maps as I had to be on my travels thru many countries in europe. I variously used and combined railroad atlas maps, train station maps, schematic rail maps, guidebook maps, city and regional and country maps, rental car city maps, bus maps, etc. For free maps check out bus and train stations, public libraries, tourist info centers, and car rental

agencies. Often(it varies from country to country) cities and towns post maps of the city and region in public places, train stations, bus stops, etc. Sometimes I'd just shell out for a good quality tourist, city, or country map when I needed extra detail to find friends, addresses, or when I was doing an extra amount of train research. Why so much mappage? Remember that written

or word of mouth train info from friends, hobos and tramps, train workers, crew change guides, and even the internet are practically non-existant in europe, further complicated by foreign languages and cultures, unfamiliar place names and complex rail systems. You'll have to make up for that with yur own intuition, experience, some leg work and plenty of maps.

SCOPING IT OUT:

How to get started? The multiplicity of yards and rail lines in european cities and towns, combined with less than great information and skimpy map resources, can be quite confusing. Like the states, sometimes important freight yards are in the industrial areas, way out on the outskirts of cities or even in much smaller outlying towns miles from the main city. If yur stuck and unsure of about where to catch a freight train, either starting out or in the midst of a freight journey, here's a handy tactics Get as many maps as you can of the city yur in and when possible, the region. Starting at the main train station(s), ride passenger trains just one or 2 or 3 stops out on each line, carefully noting freight yards, sidings, crew change spots, where lines branch or merge, stopped freight trains, etc. The frequency of passenger train service in most places makes for easy out and easy return, plus you can sightsee, plus you can practice yur passenger train scamming. You may have already discovered this while scamming trains for longer distances, but it's unusual for the conductor or ticket takers to come around for the first couple of stops- maybe yur good for ten or fifteen minutes or longer, plenty enough time to get on and ride and check out miles of track and get off with no problems. Using what maps you have and this type of traveling research you can easily piece together a somewhat comprehensive picture of what and where you can get started. All in a couple of hours, a half day or even a whole day. Take notes and mark yur maps. I found foreign place names quickly disappeared out of my head unless I wrote them down.

PLACARDS:

Just when things seem confusing or impossible, along comes a freight train with signs on it telling where it's going. Yes, european freight cars have paper placards with dates, code numbers, sometimes, type of cargo, originating point and destination. At first glance this is a little bit of hobo "big rock candy mountain" staring you in the face, and so it is. Like everything else, though, it takes some work and research. In some places they're consistant about changing and updating the placards (like switzerland), others, they're more lax about it (like spain). Some freight cars you'll see them, others not-for instance, for some reason container flats often didn't have them. Interpreting placards has it's challenges; How old is it? Is it faded and wrinkly and obviously or not so obviously out of date? Did it just go thru a rainstorm and looks old but isn't? Is the freight car empty and returning to its originating point? Or full, going to the destination point? By looking at the springs near the wheels you can sometimes tell if a freight car is loaded or empty. Is the particular car or train in the arrivals yard waiting to be broken up and reconfigured before heading out again? Or is it ready to hit the road? Foreign languages and place names, as well as differing placard designs from place to place further complicate this otherwise nice rail riding convenience. Why would there be confusion about originating and destination points, you might ask? There are thousands of cities and towns in europe, many of them with multiple freight yards, or if nothing else, delivery points. For every familiar city name I saw on a placard, I'd see ten that I didn't recognize. A certain amount of "detective" work with country maps, ideally, the kind with city and town indexes can help a lot. Sometimes(especially in big freight yards) my tactic was to leave my pack hidden somewhere safe, sneak into the yard with pen and paper, and at night a flashlite, and write down names from the placards, the track number and type of train(so I could remember later) and go back to somewhere out of the way and safe and pour over maps and map indexes, locate destinations and originating points and make decisions accordingly. Other times with small yards and less chance of being seen or busted I'd just note the placards as I walked along checking out the direction of the train, rideable cars, etc.

swiss train worker changing a placard on a boxcar

OUT OF SERVICE PASSENGER CARS:

Because passenger trains are often parked in freight yards and freights go thru and sometimes stop in passenger stations, you can wait and hide in "out of service" passenger cars and trains, either in between on the ground or more hidden in the cars themselves. Be on the alert and ready to move fast if yur freight comes in or starts moving out(remember freights can quickly reach un-catchable speed). As well, be ready to move out fast if the area or the train yur in is approached by workers or cleaning crews or it goes into service. For these reasons it's not a good idea to sleep or set up camp in a passenger car unless it's obviously abandoned.

ABANDONED PASSENGER AND FREIGHT CARS AND LOCOMOTIVES:

are quite common to see in freight yards and near train stations. These can be handy camping, hiding and waiting to catch out spots when weather is threatening or other hiding/ waiting spots are too visible or are otherwise not working out. It became second nature for me to look for these as I travelled around.

SO ITALIAN!

"Gilad, I think this guy's gonna be cool, look his shirt tail's hanging out."

Having criss-crossed my way around a bit, now in italy for the second time, I was feeling confident and somewhat expert at both the freight train scene and scamming passenger trains. Yet, spite of dozens of encounters, ticket takers still did make me a bit nervous. Even at the best of times they can be...uncomfortable. Often (in some countries), if you can't show a ticket or money yur ass gets kicked off the train. I'd invented this game called "the Good/Bad Conductor game"- something to occupy the brain for those few nervous moments as the ticket taker works their way down the isle: "Let's see,oh yeah...a pony tail,bet this one's hip." etc,etc.

So,this italian train;this conductor's coming along, Gilad's new to this being mostly a law abiding citizen, but my experienced eye takes in, besides one shirt tail hanging out, the five day old beard (a good sign) and so it's a good bet this guy's not gonna care much about a couple of ticketless ragamuffins like us, may even let us ride on? Cross yur fingers.

I'd gotten spoiled on french trains. There,the usual routine is: Ticket please. No ticket? You must pay. No money? Passport please, where are you going? Then yur issued an infraction ticket that's good for the remainder of the ride and a sixty two euro fine to be paid when you win the lottery. Like I said, spoiled.

Slovenly train conductor reaches our butt end of the car. What? No ticket? What? No money? Gestures. Passports? Ahhh,California! Now he's angry in italian. Okay, I've bombed the game badly. He's being "Bad" conductor! What's more, it's contagous already- other passengers are getting involved, scowling and muttering. No translation needed here, "How dare some americanos, Californios, no less, ride around italy for free?!" We hang our heads. More gesturing. Squirming on our part, Gilads' spanish italian isn't impressing anyone. We get the boot at the next stop, none too soon, now the passengers have us for paint bombing Michealangelos' tomb and riding for free! We're truly and properly ashamed, shit howdy! Kicked off the train we cool our jets and dumbster dive the quaint little city. Sips of free beer we found and the absurdum of bumping into and chatting with mormons from south america. We begin to laugh and slap our knees. Ugh! This will go down as one of the two most agitated conductors I run into in my six months of travel...and the most hilarios...in retrospect, of course.

Italo-phile friends tell me, "Oh, that's just him being italian, his manhood and pride required a bit of a show, everything's chill." Oh,yes...we are, after all in the land of "Ciao". ###

Thieves rob train at fake stop signal

ROME (AP) — Thieves used a homemade stoplight yesterday to rob an Italian freight train loaded with cigarettes craved by black marketeers.

The holdup was the third robbery of a freight train carrying ciga- ... Italian news reports

... the Sicily-bound train to halt.

The gang made off with about 2 tons of cigarettes legally manufactured by Italy's state tobacco monopoly and loaded them onto a truck. Police began searching for the bandits and found the truck — along with its cargo — abandoned not far away, authorities said.

Many Italian smokers feed their nicotine habit with contraband cigarettes bought from black-market vendors.

Many Italian smokers feed their nicotine habit with contraband cigarettes bought on the st... from black-mark... vend...

RIDING THE PLUSH (PASSENGER TRAIN SCAMS)

Even with excellent hobo luck and easy hitch hiking as well as other types of transpo, you'll occasionally want to ride a passenger train. I was averaging three or four passenger trains for every freight train that I rode. In most european countries you can find trains to just about anywhere and often. In large and medium sized cities, trains are coming and going constantly, in smaller cities and towns, there are dozens of trains a day. If yur on a limited budget and need to play the scam game, euro train systems are for you. The make up of trains, their priority, speed, configuration, style, conductor/ ticket taker behavior, ease of scamability or not, can differ greatly region to region, country to country. My advice on free riding is do yur homework-similar to freight hopping, scaming the passeger systems of europe will require some "detective

work and some smarts. Spend the neccesary time and energy in train stations, on and off the trains to figure out patterns and what works best? What kind of trains do what? There are big differences between intra-country, express, commuter, and regional trains. What might the differences be with ease of scamability between large and medium and small train stations? What are the best tactics for getting on the least suspiciously and then moving from car to car to distance yurself from the ticket taker(s) or "controllers" as they're called in some places? Where do they get off and re-board the train-the back, middle, or front end? Are some platforms in the stations easier to hang out on and blend into the crowds away from the prying eyes of security people? Some train stations at different times require a ticket just to get thru to the platforms, is there a way around that or should you buy a cheap ticket so as to get onto the platforms(this wasn't that common of a situation)? Is the causual approach best or is it better to pull the quick get on when train personel aren't looking or absent for the moment? Are there front end or butt end compartments that they may not check or notice you in? I rode relaxed and somewhat hidden in these ticket free spaces many times with little or no problems. Are there bike cars on some trains where ticket takers rarely visit? These were common, for instance, in italy. Keep yur eyes open for "honor system" pay-at-the-machine regional type trains with most often no ticket takers at all? I rode dozens of these hassle free, for example, in switzerland, where they are common. A note here about bathroom scams: I never did it, somehow that level of clausterphobic hiding plus missing much of scenery didn't appeal to me, but for those so inclined, hiding in the bathrooms of trains can apparently work. I paid a lot of attention to reading and interpretating train schedules, both the kind you put in yur pocket and the posted schedules around the stations. Schedules can give good clues on how and what to try and scam, and combined with city and regional and country maps can make it easier to know directions, transfer points, destinations. Keep yur wits about you and figure ahead of time where you wanna switch trains, alternative routes, or do damage control when you get kicked off, etc. Hanging out at

stations can also double as valuable time spent noting and figuring out freight train traffic as well. If yur light on yur feet and decisive, you can switch between freight riding and passenger trains relatively easy(sometimes)as the sitch requires.

ATTITUDE

Large and smaller details aside, much of my travel experience had a sometime subtle and other times, a blatant overlay of what might be labeled (for lack of a better phrase) "travel attitude". To varying degrees, train personel, security guards and cops, border police, even some citizens take

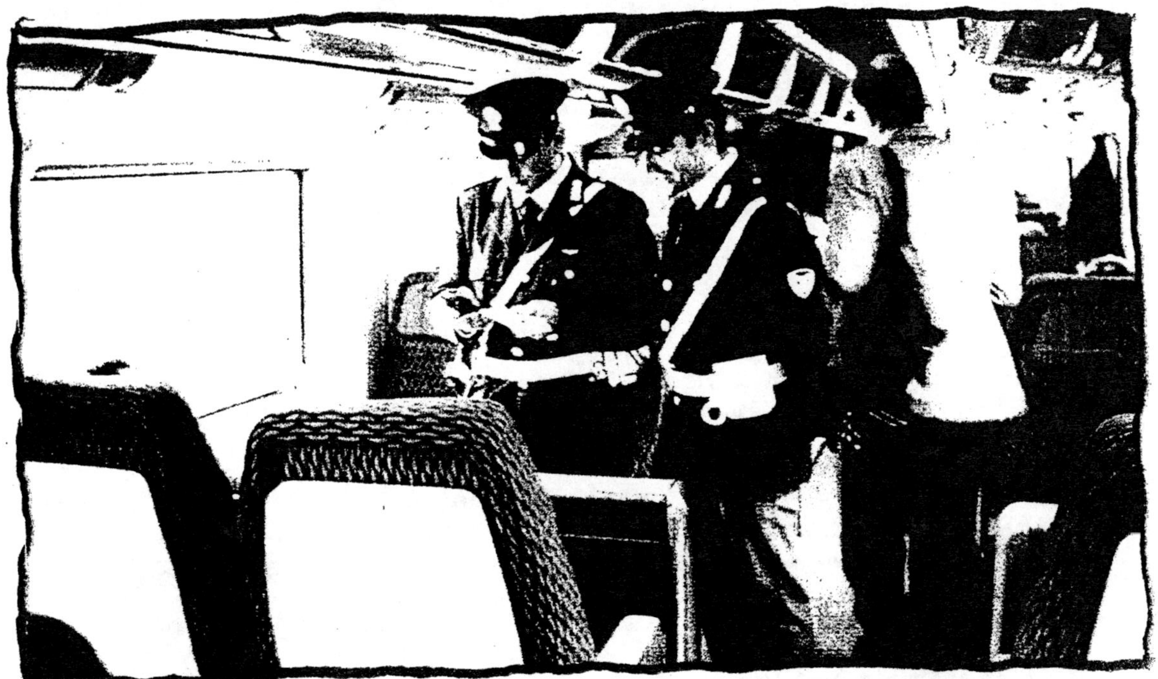

scaming passenger trains seriously and I suppose same applies to freight hopping(though, I never got caught doing that). If you play the scam game, you'll, sooner or later, encounter attempts to extract the price of a ticket (usually more, once yur on the train), or a fine, or you can be issued an infraction ticket, to be paid later(this was common in france). These can be accompanied by lectures, frowns, finger shaking, head wagging, and bad feelings. My attitudes about scaming evolved over time, but were always based on my personal want and need and philosophy to be able to wander freely on a very limited budget. If you do it, do it without shame or embarassment and with respect for others. Everybody has their own style, some people do "the crying game" or the "the lying game" and maybe it works for them? I disliked the need to act out that level of dishonesty and victim mentality. I tried to keep two things in mind while scamming europe- one: it might seem odd to americans where we've a prevailing culture of "looking out for number one", getting ahead and taking advantage by any means...it's prevalent in punk culture all the way up to the rich and politically powerful in america, but in many european countries they've created admirably honest societies. I remind myself, I'm a guest here. And, two: even though I have strong feelings of "belonging" to the trains. I'm also the guest of the conductor and other train personel, I'm on their "territory". I tried, in my own way, to honor those things in europe and on the trains. In short; don't be another ugly american! Likewise, punk rock rudeness and self-righteous anarchy don't cut it here either. Yeah, we all know we're citizens of the world, fuck borders, the trains are ours for the taking, etc. but no one will be helped, least of all, you, by coping an attitude, many times train workers turned a blind eye to me being where I wasn't supposed to be, conductors let me ride when they could have kicked me off. I had decent and even friendly chats with conductors after they busted me and hopefully, left them with a pleasant impression of train scammers and tramps. Also, that americans don't have to be jerks (as we are currently percieved to be by many europeans). Occasionally, conductors got worked up, coped attitude or were unneccesarily disdainful, etc. Still, I found friendliness and respectfulness left me feeling okay and maybe would smooth things out for the next no-budget traveler. For sustainable scam travel, I preferred the honest & confident approach... practical things are you blend in and are less suspicious or hesitant in making yur moves, and encounters when you are caught, will go better. If yur act isn't already dirtied up, you might wanna do so- it'll be more believable that yur a poverty case. The downside, of course, is if yur raggedy, dusty, and patched punk you'll stand out more. In spite of the "straight-up" attitude and the free ride, sometimes there's an emotional price to pay... occasional "bad" days with not much progress, several busts, especially if there were unfriendly feelings, embarassment at getting caught, etc. I would just stop, switch over to freight trains, camp out, lick my wounds and try again... later. On "good" days and they were many, I traveled for hundreds and thousands of kilometers without problems. ##

STREET SMARTS

BUSES

Be prepared to pay when you must or when it would be obnoxios but with some buses and transit bus systems you can ride free if it's an "honor" system or by entering and exiting the rear doors, etc. Watch for "controllers"(rare) who can issue infractions.

CAMPING

The idea of non-paying "roughing it" style camping is unusual, even seen as odd but laxer attitudes about trespassing make it generally easy. With minimal problemo I camped in parks,polo grounds,caves, factories,beaches,orchards, the mountains,garden sheds, abandoned houses, etc. etc.

METRIC

Europe (and the rest of the world) have funny measurements which can be confusing to the average american. Most of it is not worth bothering yur head about, except to remember that a liter is close enough to a quart to be the same (gas pumps, for instance measure by liters instead of gallons). A kilo is about 2 pounds, a little more. A kilometer is .621 of a mile, which sounds confusing but sweetly, works out to very close to 5/8s of a mile. Trains in europe, of course, use "kilometer posts" instead of mile posts- you'll get used to these whizzing by and remembering the 5/8s of a mile rule, you'll quickly become familiar and accurate with figuring distances with barely a second thought.

railroad bulls may look mean in europe but they're not so bad

CRIME

We're so used to thinking of ourselves as the criminals, huh? What are the dangers that the poor non-touristy, train hopper type might encounter? Violence? Rape? Robbery? It's my on-going impression that western, northern, and southern europe are much less violent cultures than america, less violent crime, safer and more respectful, and because of that less paranoid and fearful. These are large and impressive societal differences between america (and other places in the world) and europe! Nonetheless, as anywhere, self defense skills can be handy. Hone yur skills at being a good judge of character and situation. Keep yur money hidden well. Be streetwise and smart, and likely you'll have little or no problems.

DUMBSTERS

Plentitude of dumbstered food varied wildly. Wealthier contries throw away more food than poorer countries. I had the best consistant luck in england, switzerland, and somewhat to my surprise, greece. Organic (or "Bio" as it's universally known by here)can be quite common in some store dumbsters. The best cheese I had in france came out of the trash.

FLYING FOR CHEAP

Check out "Ryan Air" and other similar airlines for intra-country, surprisingly cheap flights to and from england and all over the continent.

FARMERS AND STREET MARKETS

Besides being able to buy good quality, and often organic, produce you can also score and eat the perfectly good throw-aways (tons of it) as the mar-kets close or just by asking.

FERRIES

I rode five of them in italy and greece and england/france and never got a clue about how to stowaway on them, good luck.

friendly traveller punk kid I hung out with in a french freight yard

FESTIVALS

Pagans,hippies,punks,ravers and nomads all regurely get together for huge rural music fests thru-out europe- no real equivalent of it in the states, but a big part of D.I.Y. culture there.

HOSTELS Aren't they 'sposed to be cheap traveller crash pads? Too expensive for my tastes. If you need a shower and the occasional night in the soft bed (during bad weather?) cheapo and/or fleabag hotels can be inexpensive.

LANGUAGE English is both the generally accepted common and bizness language in most countries, americanos will mostly get by fine with no secondary languages. Knowing a little or a lot of german, french, spanish, italian or other euro languages wont hurt though. Freight train and yard workers didn't often speak english (was it some working class thing?) but passenger train people usually knew some or a lot.

METROS The cost of inner city, outer city, and longer distance regional metros can quickly add up. Cutting yur travel costs on these can include going around, "doubling up", or jumping turnstyles and barriers. If you can't get into "the system" easily, pay for short distance and ride long distance. Watch for metro agents, cameras, and security and get around them when possible. Some station agents have their back turned, or are absent, or can be distracted. Maybe they don't care or don't see it as their job to bust free riders. Some stations are open access (without turnstyles or gates). Sometimes sympathetic passengers may help you thru the turnstyles. When caught, similar to freight and passenger trains, what can happen? Expect some interogation, lecturing, and attempts to give infractions or fines. Plead poverty and (hopefully) go on yur way.

MONEY The european union (E.U.) which is the majority of countries there has universalized money- the "euro" makes for a lot less confusion and money changing than in the past. I dislike banks and tried to minimize my contact with them. As well, I disdain travellers checks. If yur of a similar bent here's a few old hobo tricks: keep money hidden in a few different places on yur body and backpack. I kept the majority of my cash- 'merican, swiss, english, and the euro (switzerland and england aren't in the E.U.) in waterproof baggies under the insoles of my hobo boots which should be hidden or act as yur pillow when asleep, safe and secure.

NOMADS Keep yur eyes open for these folks, whole caravans of nomads in buses, campers, trucks, and cars tour england and the continent. Along with the many festivals these are shared roaming communities where punks, hippies, pagans, activists, travellers and like minded folk mingle and travel together.

PAY FOR TRAINS Flexibility is an essential aspect of low-bagger travel and even the most scam wise traveller must occasionally shell out for a train ride. For instance, in greece, where passenger trains were few and far between it became apparent that free rides and scams that had worked elsewhere just weren't happening there. Yur mostly travelling on the cheap and sometimes you gotta pay a little and thats okay.

SQUATS

Squatter laws are remarkably tolerant and progressive. The urban squatter scene is alive and well and quite impressive in many cities. A lot of american and foreign anarchists, punks, and activists connect up with their european counterparts in the squat communities- a place to stay and connect up with people, learn about anarchism euro style and contibute to true D.I.Y. (do-it-yurself) living. Unfortunatly, freight hopping and hobo lifestyle, being unknown in western europe: the two things didn't match up for me with the exception to some good exposure to the london squat scene and some friends there. 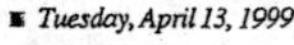

Tuesday, April 13, 1999

Associated Press

The two cars of an elevated train lie in the Wupper River after falling during the morning commute. The derailment is being blamed on a metal clamp that apparently was left on the track after weekend construction.

STANDARD DISCLAIMER

Three dead, 47 injured as German train derails

An advertisement for riding freight 'stead of passenger trains? In any case, hoboing on freight trains in europe is illegal and as potentially danger-ous (and maybe, more so) as anywhere else in the world. This zine is for entertainment purposes, only! Nothing here is in-tended to encourage or discourage anyone from doing dangerous, illegal activities, blah, blah, blah. Enjoy. Be safe.

"HEY, HOW DO YOU SAY 'HUMP YARD' IN GERMAN?"

Imagine, yur slinking thru the berlin freight yards one night and you run smack into a worker- the hiding game is up. Normally, not knowing any german you'd mutter and putter and both of you would be worse for wear. But thanx to these few railroad phrases, now, you could with confidence, stroll up and belt out with "Hey, are those Spezialflachwagen fur den Transport von Schwerfahrzeugen (piggyback car) going into the Empfangsgleise (recieving yard) or are they on the Ausfahrgleis (outbound track)?" Just for a litle bit of american flair you can throw in "Ich bin ein Berliner! (I'm a jelly donut!)"

There's two hundred languages in europe(they say) but I thot these four commonly spoken ones might make train travel a little easier. I spent days in paris trying to find both the actual thing and the word for freight yard! Language can be frustrating. Keep in mind these are the formal words- likely there's common words and even slang that common folk and train workers use that are variations or are different. Hope this helps.

	SPANISH	FRENCH	GERMAN	ITALIAN
AUTOMOBLE CAR	vagón para automoviles	wagon porte-automobiles	Autotran-spotwagen	carro bisarca
BOXCAR	vagón cerrado	wagon couvert	Drehge stellwaggon	carro merci chiuso
CLASSIFI-CATION YARD	zona de clasificacion	zone de triage	Ordnungsgeis	area di smistamento
COMMUTER TRAIN	tren suburbano	train de banlieue	Nahver kehszug	treno locale
CONTAINER	contenedor	conteneur	Container	container
CONTAINER CAR	vagón para contenedores	wagon porte-conteneurs	Container flachwagen	carro pianale portacontainer

	SPANISH	FRENCH	GERMAN	ITALIAN
COUPLER KNUCKLE	rotula de enganche	mâchoire d'attelage	Herzstück	gancio di trazione
DESTINATION	destinos	destination	Zielbahnhof	destiazione
FLAT CAR	plataforma	wagon plat	Drehgestell-flachwagen	carro pianale
FREIGHT CAR	vagón de carga	wagon	Güterwagen	carro merci
FREIGHT STATION	estacion de carga	gare de marchandises	Güterbahnhof	scalo merci
GONDOLA CAR	vagón de mercancias	wagon tombereau	offener Güterwagen	carro scoperto a sponde basse
HOPPER CAR	vagón tolva	wagon tremie	Bodenen-tieererwagen	carro a tramoggia
HOPPER ORE CAR	vagón tolva para minerales	wagon tremie à mineral	Schutt gutwagen	carro a tramoggia per mineralli
HUMP	terraplén de desenganche	butte de dëbranchement	Ablaufberg	pangina
LOCOMOTIVE	locomotora	locomotive	Lokomotive	locomotiva
MAIN LINE	via principal	grandes lignes	Hauptgleis	linea ferroviaria principale
OUTBOUND TRACK	via de salida	voie de sortie	Ausfahrgleis	binario di uscita
PASSENGER CAR	vagón de pasajeros	voiture	Mittelwagen	carrozza passeggeri
PASSENGER STATION	estación de ferrocarril	gare de voyageurs	Personen-bahnhof	stazione dei viaggiatori
PASSENGER TRAIN	tren de pasajeros	train	Reisezug	treno passeggen
PIGGYBACK CAR	plataforma para transpotar vagones	wagon rail route	Spezialflack-wagen für den Transport von Schwerfahrzeugen	carro pianale per li trasporto di rimorchi
RAILROAD TRACK	via férrea	voie ferrée	Eisenbahn-Oberbau	strada ferrata

	SPANISH	FRENCH	GERMAN	ITALIAN
RECIEVING YARD	zona de recepción	zone de réception	Empfangs-gleise	area ricevitrice
ROUTING CARDBOARD PLACARD	tarjeta de ruta	porte-étiquette d'acheminement	Wagen-laufschild	cartellino indicatore di destinazione
SCHEDULES	horarios	tableau horaire	Kursbuchtafein	orari
SIGNAL	semáforo	sémaphore	Signal	semaforo
SUBWAY MAP	mapa de rutas	carte de réseau	U-Bahn Netzplan	carta della rete metro-politana
SUBWAY STATION	estación de metro	station de metro	U-Bahn Station	stazione della metropolitana
SUBWAY TRAIN	tren subterráneo	rame de métro	U-Bahn Zug	treno della metropolitana
SWITCH TOWER	torre de señales	poste d'aiguillage	Stellwerk	cabina di manovra
TANK CAR	vagón cisterna	wagon citerne	Kesselwagen	carro cisterna
TICKET COLLECTOR	revisor	contrôleur	Fahrkarten-kontrolleur	controllore
TUNNEL	túnel	tunnel	Tunnel	galleria

###

hiding in a well car spanish/french border

Shreya, hoboerotica, abandoned rail line
Sierra Nevada, Spain

More railroad glory from www.Microcosm.Pub

Keep your rollin' parties going at www.Microcosm.Pub